Sailing INTO THE LIGHT

SUSAN HIGHSMITH

ILLUSTRATED BY ROBERTA ROGERS

Words Matter Publishing
P. O. Box 1190
Decatur, IL 62525
www.wordsmatterpublishing.com

ISBN: 978-1-962467-09-4

Library of Congress Catalog Card Number: 2023946163

For all those who have taken

this journey in physical form,

and are now ready to embark

on the next journey.

Acknowledgement

I have been inspired by the transitions of several Beloved Souls. Some I was able to sit with while they were passing into the next Dimension. Some left this Earthly Plane before I could say "good-bye." I do so now with great love and appreciation for their Presences in my life: Tommy Highsmith, Barbara Findeisen, Ray Castellino, Kathy Starr, Penny Peterson Nagel, Barbara Grainger, Bonnie Grainger, Caroline Pentacost, both my parents Wayne and Betty Perske, and Dick Pino. For the steadfast support my husband Charles provides, I am deeply grateful. For the magnificent artistry of my friend Roberta Rogers, I am awed and appreciative. To my precious granddaughter Lindsay who listened and shared her counsel, I treasure her suggestions and assistance. My family has so unfailingly supported my writing and encouraged me in all my endeavors—you are valued beyond measure.

Prologue

Many people have been inspired, as I was, by the poem *Gone from my Sight* written in the 1800s by Henry Van Dyke. I share this treasure with you here.

I am standing upon the seashore.
A ship at my side spreads her white sails to the morning breeze,
and starts for the blue ocean.
She is an object of beauty and strength,
and I stand and watch her until she hangs like a speck of white cloud
just where the sea and sky come down to meet and mingle with each other.
Then someone at my side says: "There! She's gone!"
Gone where? Gone from my sight—that is all.
She is just as large in mast and hull and spar as she was when she left my side,
and just as able to bear her load of living freight
to the place of her destination.
Her diminished size is in me and not in her.

And just at that moment
when someone at my side says: "There! She's gone!"
there are other eyes that are watching for her coming;
and other voices ready to take up the glad shout:
"There she comes!"

And that is—"dying."

In recent years I have "lost" a number of Loved Ones. I realize they are not "lost" at all. They have left their bodies and the Essence of who they are—their Spirits—have moved on to a different, and, in my belief, a kinder world. After my son Tommy passed, he came to me in Spirit and told me that there was "only unconditional love" where he was. I am eternally grateful to have that reassurance. I hold that belief in Everlasting Love for everyone.

This book is intended to be read by caregivers to anyone who is transitioning into the next Life. It can be read in Hospices, care facilities, or at home with a Loved One. The story is a modern metaphor designed to ease any fears that one may have as he or she lays down the garment worn during physical embodiment. Perhaps envisioning a boat with billowing sails approaching a distant shore can be reassuring to those who take this journey. Perhaps they can hear those voices of Loved Ones welcoming them home. People who have had near death experiences report the beauty, love and light they felt in that Realm. The poem *Gone from my Sight* is frequently read at a funeral, after a loved one has passed. Would it not be wiser to share the sentiment with them *before* they go? Might it ease their transition? It is my wish that each Precious Soul know Peace and Infinite Love as they begin their ultimate journey—and welcome us when it is our time to join them.

Not just once, but many times, and not just long ago but even now, sailboats rest easy, anchored in a calm harbor.

It's late in the day. Clouds gently float in front of the sun, creating a pink and golden yellow veil as the globe settles down for the night.

A small boat rests on the emerald
water, sensing the ebb and flow of the
tides as she rises and falls with the slow
rhythm of the sea.

She gazes at the luminescent
moon lifting off the horizon.
What great force elevates this
shimmering sphere? she wonders.

What energy causes the vast ocean to caress the shore, then shyly retreat?

What great power blows
the wind through my sails
and carries me to strange lands?

I have sailed through many
turbulent seas and I have navigated
them all, she recalls.

I have raced with others
and, many times, I have
won the race.

I know this trip will be my last,
but I'm eager to embark on this
new journey. She tests the wind
with her sails.

Standing on the dock
are well-wishers.

She breathes the glorious
breeze into her sails and lets go
of her anchor line.

A puff of wind fills her sails and
she moves on slippery waves to deeper
sapphire blue waters.

Traveling more quickly now,
she hears her friends on the shore say,
"There she goes."

Keeping her focus on
the rising full moon, she feels its
light embracing her.

She can hear whispers calling
to her from another shore.
A chorus begins to sing their welcome,
"Here she comes."

She surrenders to the force of the mighty wind, and she is carried forth to a new welcoming land.

www.ingramcontent.com/pod-product-compliance
Lightning Source LLC
Chambersburg PA
CBHW041129120626
46547CB00019B/2912